Having worked with the consumers of land since 1987, I know that the concepts outlined in this book are absolutely crucial to creating the financing certainty and flexibility required in the ever-changing landscape of master-planned community development.

—Greg Vogel
Founder and CEO, Land Advisors Organization

If you are actively involved in the development of residential communities in the complex and costly environment which is California, *Land to Lots*™ is a must-read. The concepts outlined in the book, if taken to heart and utilized, can result in significant differences to a project's bottom-line results.

—Jeff Spindler
Founding Principal and President of Land Advisors Organization, California Division

The concepts and tools that have been masterfully captured in the pages of this book are the cornerstone of financing and developing master-planned communities. A must-read for everyone in the master-planned development industry.

—Michael Baldwin
Senior Vice President, Jefferies

The concepts outlined in this book are major linch-pins in the successful development of any large-scale master-planned community.

—Dan Kelly
Chief Operating Officer, DMB Associates, Inc.

If you are a land investor, developer, or home builder you have to read this book. The tools and concepts outlined are exactly what every developer must recognize and put into play to facilitate the development of increasingly more complex and costly residential communities.

—Tim Green
Director, Coats Rose

This book is a great roadmap for clients looking at creative financing alternatives and ways to supercharge their project returns. A must-read for anyone in the development industry!

—Brian Rosener
President and COO, Land Advisors Organization

Land to Lots™

Land to Lots™

HOW TO BORROW MONEY YOU DON'T HAVE TO PAY BACK AND LAUNCH MASTER PLANNED COMMUNITIES

CARTER FROELICH

ethos
collective

Printed in the United States of America

Published by Ethos Collective™
PO Box 43
Powell, OH 43065

Library of Congress Cataloging: 2023902391

Softcover: 978-1-63680-131-5

Hardcover: 978-1-63680-132-2

E-book: 978-1-63680-133-9

Available in hardcover, softcover, and e-book.

Dedication

This book is dedicated to all the professionals in the development and home-building industry striving to produce thoughtful and meaningful places.

Contents

Part 4—Countdown

Appendices

INTRODUCTION

Borrow Money You Don't Have to Pay Back

I started on this journey I'm about to take you on by working with my company, Launch Development Finance Advisors. We've been around in some form or another since the mid-eighties when I started working with an accounting firm by the name of Kenneth Leventhal in their Orange County office in southern California.

Launch solely represents the private sector in matters of public finance, which means we work with land developers, commercial developers, and home builders to help them with financing infrastructure. We also assist our clients in the reduction of infrastructure costs and the mitigation of risk, all to optimize project returns. As an affiliate of the Land Advisors Organization, the largest land-only brokerage firm in the United States, our goal has always been to be a hero to the land development and home-building industries. With that big goal in mind, Launch has established several unique processes to help our clients accelerate cash into their pro forma cash flow and to maximize their project's financial returns.

Real estate entrepreneurs have a growing number of challenges that I'll be shedding some light on throughout this book:

- escalating costs of land, materials, labor, and financing costs

- increasingly demanding jurisdictional requirements

- ever-increasing development impact fees and exactions

With costs for everything in this industry consistently rising, we recognized that real estate entrepreneurs like you needed another way to finance your projects and grow your businesses. What better way to do that than borrowing money you don't have to pay back?

This all happens through special district financing.

This type of financing involves the issuance of tax-exempt bonds to finance public improvements within a specified geographical area, or district. Districts may construct public improvements and/or purchase public improvements that have been constructed by the developer through bond proceeds. The bonds are repaid from the special taxes, assessments, and/or an *ad valorem* property tax imposed on the land within the district. Property owners in the district finance the improvements without any city-wide or county-wide taxpayer subsidy. The bonds are typically underwritten in limited public offerings managed by underwriting firms that specialize in this type of land-secured financing.

Various state statutes provide authorization for special district financing. The nomenclature for special district varies according to location, but some of the more common names include metropolitan districts (metro districts), municipal utility districts (MUD), public improvement districts (PID), special improvement districts (SID), special assessment districts (SAD), community facility districts (CFD), improvement districts (ID), community development districts (CDD), and tax increment financing districts (TIF).

The infrastructure for which special district financing may be used is defined by state statute. In some jurisdictions, they are also used to fund specific public services, such as water and sewer services, public safety, snow removal, street cleaning, and maintenance of the infrastructure.

Commonly, most special districts are allowed to finance public water and sewer systems, public roadways and other transportation improvements, drainage projects, public safety facilities, and equipment, as well as public parks and recreational facilities. The determination of what special district to utilize is dependent upon many factors including but not limited to:

1. special districts allowable under state law in which the project is located

2. jurisdictional policies related to the use of districts

3. the type of public infrastructure allowed to be financed by state-enabling statutes

4. the phasing schedule of the project

5. other available financing resources

6. the competitive environment

Special districts are typically, but not always, separate political subdivisions from the jurisdiction that creates the special district. The obligation to repay these bonds is passed on to the end users of the property located within the special district's boundaries.

Based upon the type and location, the district may issue general obligation, revenue, special assessment, and/or special tax bonds to finance eligible public improvements.

The bonds issued typically have terms ranging from twenty to forty years, with tax-exempt interest rates ranging from 3 to 7 percent. Typically, the only security for the bonds is the property located within the special district itself—no other forms of developer financial assurance or guarantees are required. As the special district is typically a separate political subdivision from that of the establishing jurisdiction, the establishing jurisdiction does not have to repay bondholders should the developer or property owners default on their debt obligations.

A special district's *ad valorem* taxes, special assessments, or special taxes are imposed in addition to the traditional jurisdictional statutory property taxes on real property and are authorized for a specific period to fund specific improvements. Depending on the type of bond being issued, future homeowners will repay the bonds through the payment of additional *ad valorem* taxes in the case of general obligation bonds, special assessment payments in the case of special assessment bonds, or special tax levies in the case of special tax bonds. Sales taxes, various excise taxes, and/or user fees can also be utilized to support special district revenue bond financing to the extent allowed by specific states enabling legislation.

Special district *ad valorem*, special assessments, and special taxes carry the same priority as real property tax, meaning that in the case of delinquency or non-payment, the collection is enforced in the same manner as real property taxes. Because real property taxes have precedence over private liens, including mortgages, the governmental entity and the special district have the right to foreclose on the land securing the bond obligation and ultimately collecting delinquent amounts by a tax sale of the property.

Public hearings are necessary to establish special districts, and disclosure and notification of the existence of the district in real estate contracts, deeds, or marketing materials to purchasers of property may be required by enabling legislation or policy guidelines published by the governmental entity.

Every Deal Is Different.

At Launch, I've worked on deals for land that range from 5 acres to 56,000 acres. Though each project might be completely different from the next one, I utilize these 5 concepts that sit at the foundation of handcrafting successful financing:

- determining a Path & Plan™
- creating certainty
- creating flexibility
- reducing, eliminating, and/or deferring infrastructure costs
- accelerating cash into the pro forma.

But, before we dive into these concepts, I want to give you a bit of a background about how these concepts came into our company.

When I was moving out of the audit department at Kenneth Leventhal & Company, there was a group of us making a move into the management consulting department of the firm. Right around this time,

California enacted Proposition 13, which dried up the revenues cities could collect through their property taxes. This huge change, almost seeming to happen overnight, limited the amount of taxes that jurisdictions could collect to 1 percent of a property's assessed value.

The cities suddenly announced they had no money to build the infrastructure for real estate developers, so now it was the developers' responsibility to fund and build all the necessary infrastructure. The development community responded swiftly, asking for permission to finance the infrastructure as though they were a jurisdiction. So, in 1982, Senator Henry Mello and Assemblyman Mike Roos helped pass the Mello-Roos Community Facilities District Act of 1982 (Mello-Roos Act).

The Mello-Roos Act allowed developers to set up special-purpose taxing districts over their master-planned communities and/or subdivisions, and these CFDs would issue tax-exempt bonds to fund the required public improvements. Those bonds were paid back by a special tax levy placed on the land contained within the boundaries of the district. So, we—the newly minted management consultants Kenneth Leventhal asked to read the Mello-Roos Act—thought to ourselves, *Let's see if we've got this right.*

Under one scenario, we can borrow $200 million from a third-party bank and pay that money back with points and interest over time. Alternatively, we can borrow that same $200 million through the establishment of a CFD and essentially pass the obligations to repay the CFD bond obligations to the homeowners. And we said, "Hell, we don't even need a calculator to figure this out—let's start doing it!" And that's exactly what we did. We started setting up some of the first CFDs in the state of California for the large ranch owners and landowners based in Orange County and San Diego County. And we've been doing that ever since, not only in California but around the country.

To date, Launch is currently practicing in several different states, primarily Arizona, California, Colorado, Florida, Idaho, Nevada, New Mexico, Texas, and Utah. We've been involved in the issuance of billions of dollars of bonds. And we've established hundreds of districts in all these different states.

When I presented this idea to one of our clients, they thought it was impossible. They thought there was no way to borrow without having to pay it back— in fact, they used the term "alchemy." I cannot tell you how many different times I met with this client to explain the concept. I had to show this developer their particular state's enabling statutes and walk them through other districts and other transactions we had set up for our clients in the same state. Even after all this hand-holding, they still had a hard time wrapping their head around how they could borrow money and not have to pay it back.

What they were used to was the standard way of financing development projects—meaning, they would buy the property using their money or an equity partner's money, then they would find a third-party debt provider that would lend them the money. This borrowed money, secured by a first deed of trust on the property, would enable them to put in the public and private infrastructure—streets, roads, sewers, and storm drains. Then, as they sold parcels or finished lots to the homebuilders, they would take the proceeds from the lot sales and pay down the debt on the loan. For them, this idea of obtaining money to construct infrastructure they don't have to pay back was absolutely foreign to them. And they thought it was too good to be true.

One of the things you need to be aware of when we're talking about special purpose taxing districts is that public debt issued through the special purpose taxing districts is non-recourse debt secured by the land only. There are no corporate or personal guarantees required. Second of all, we are issuing bonds at a tax-exempt interest rate. So, what does that mean? If I'm an Arizona resident buying bonds for a project in the state of Arizona, then the interest I am paid over time on the bonds is exempt for Arizona state and federal income tax purposes.

As a result of this process, the borrowing rate is dramatically lower than what we could get through a private equity provider or an institutional bank. Typically, district bonds are issued in the 3 to 6 percent range. The bonds we're talking about as it relates to the special purpose taxing districts are long-term debt—meaning, they are paid back over a twenty-five to thirty-year time period, rather than a traditional bank loan paid back over three years.

Another consideration is that as ownership changes within the boundaries of the district, the responsibility for paying back the district debt obligation on the bonds issued changes as well. For instance, if we issue debt that's secured initially by the original land developer, and he sells a parcel to a home builder at the close of escrow, the home builder then becomes responsible for the debt obligation on the lands they have just acquired. Then, when the home builder sells lots to individual homeowners, those homeowners pay the debt obligation on their specific lot.

Later on down the road, that homeowner might sell their home to another homebuyer, then that new homebuyer steps in and starts making the debt service payments on the outstanding district debt until that bond is paid in full. Thus, when you sell the land, the obligation to repay the bonds passes on to the next landowner. So, you are not paying off that loan as you would with a traditional bank loan.

So, what happened with the developer who didn't believe in this process?

Well, they finally found their faith in this process, and they decided they were going to create one of these districts. However, they did it a little differently than we would have if they had hired us—they hired an underwriter. The underwriter set up the deal to issue more debt than what the property would support, through a target tax rate that they had established. And to do this, the underwriter talked the developer into providing corporate guarantees to service the debt above what the tax rate would typically support. As a result, they had a big influx of cash, and everything was good until the Great Recession hit. And when they couldn't sell any more homes, they couldn't pass on that debt obligation. At some point, the capitalized interest period started to burn off, and they had to write the checks on this corporate guarantee to the bondholders.

In my world, guaranteeing bonds is an absolute no-no, You never do it because it never ends up well. And if you are going to guarantee these bonds, then you need to know how you're going to get out of the transaction if you need to, or what it's going to cost you to get out of it. The developer eventually "paid" their way out of the problem. And now they're working exclusively with us moving forward, and they've never guaranteed another bond. Again, a word to the wise: Never guarantee land-secured financing!

When you enter into these types of transactions, if you're not familiar with them, it is paramount to bring in somebody who can tell you the pros and cons of the transaction. Remember that underwriters work for the bondholders—they don't work for you. They're helping you get money, but at the end of the day, their allegiance is with the bondholders and they structure their advice to favor of the bondholders.

You need someone who can represent you and only you to help craft a custom-made financing strategy that matches your business plan. Finding the right person or company will help you get as close as you possibly can to achieving that goal of living within the particular statutes that you must work with, based upon the state in which the project is located.

What we do is not alchemy. This is a proven means by which developers, home builders, and commercial developers can borrow money to fund public infrastructure through bonds passed on to the end users as the land is developed and sold to commercial users, industrial users, and home builders. Those home builders and commercial/industrial developers pass on the special district obligations to their end users. This is a proven practice since the 1970s and 1980s. At its most basic level, this practice has been utilized since local governments started building roads through the use of improvement districts in the early 1900s in the United States.

The beauty of this practice is that it reduces the amount of equity that you as a developer need to bring to the table. It can also reduce your third-party borrowing costs, therefore reducing the project's overall financing charges and enhancing your project's profitability.

The Dangers: What Keeps You Up at Night?

After you understand what vision you want to take for your project, there will likely be several challenges and obstacles you foresee. These potential pitfalls are important to pay attention to as you get to work because they will likely cause you a fair amount of stress over the next several months as you execute the Path & Plan.

Like the developer I mentioned earlier, you might feel a little skeptical about the ability of this financing technique to create success for you and your project. Perhaps, like this developer, you think the way this works sounds like alchemy, but I can assure you that there is no magic or pixie dust behind our Land to Lots™ program. It is a structured, proven way to engineer a stronger project that can reduce your financial risks and exposure.

Throughout this book, I'll address your skepticism and the other fears you may encounter as you learn more about my process for borrowing money you don't have to pay back. These are important feelings to pay attention to because understanding how to solve these internal issues are all part of what makes this technique so successful—preparation is the key, and I'll be your guide.

The Opportunities: What Are You Excited About?

But there's something else about this process that's important, too—what about your future project gets you excited? Whatever creates interest for you will propel you forward as you learn more and dive deeper into your unique Path & Plan. Acknowledging the reasons you decided to take on this project will help you build up your passion for what you're about to do.

We all need passion and drive on the projects we set out to tackle because that emotion reminds us why we started on this path. You might have moments when you feel like you're on the edge of giving up, but your passion will supply the surge of energy to start your engine again.

Likely, one of the biggest reasons you're excited about your project is because of the opportunities it will provide for you and your business. And you would be right—there are plenty of opportunities that will flow from this project as you take on the Land to Lots strategies. I'll walk you through those opportunities and teach you how to make the best decisions to optimize those opportunities for growth as they arise.

The Strengths: What Do You Bring to the Table?

Another important part of this path is recognizing what unique talents you and your company bring to the project. Those strengths will become an integral part of the formula for your future success with this project. Remember what I said above about every deal being different? You are a foundational part of what will make this deal different from others. Perhaps recognizing those strengths early on will make this project much stronger than others you've finished in the past.

This part of the process is all about building your confidence so you can see potential challenges, before you break ground, so that you can overcome them and capture opportunities that come your way. This sets you up for future success because it helps you realize you already possess the fundamental skills and talent to complete this project.

The Mantra: Helping Our Clients Achieve More.

Just like you, I work to prove my worth every day in my business with my clients—and now with you as you read the rest of this book. I truly believe each of us is only as good as our last deal. So, the work we do with every client can make or break our company. But it's not really about achieving more for Launch—it's about helping our clients achieve more through the work we do with them. That's our mission statement: *Helping Our Clients Achieve More Since 1994.*

I use an ambiguous word like "more" because what's *more* to you might be less to somebody else—or vice versa. This ambiguity gives you creative license to design the future you want for your company, and it all starts—or continues—with your next project. Maybe you want more financial returns with this project or maybe you want to create more for your community. And all that will come—better parks, technology, roads, social programming, landscaping, and/or schools. Whatever it is, you can have it—you're starting today with a blank canvas.

For the past forty-plus years, I've been in the real estate development business, and as we work through this book together, I'm going to teach you the basics of how to make my Land to Lots program work for you. I'll steer you through the rapids and guide you across rickety bridges, showing you the shortcuts that allow you to minimize your risk and maximize your returns.

I'm going to tell you things that have worked for us. I'm going to tell you things that have not worked for us. I am going to ask you to question everything that you think you know that's good. And, as we go on this journey together, we might also find other paths that haven't been taken before. This journey is all about you and the decisions you need to make along the way. However, I will do my best to lay out the Path & Plan.

When you're ready to take the path less traveled, keep reading. The journey ahead awaits you.

PART 1

Planning

1

Structuring the Plan

The work we do with our clients starts with the discovery I talked about in the introduction—the dangers, the opportunities, and the strengths. When we first meet the clients, they might not be entirely sure of what path to take for success. But, as the discovery conversations progress, we start to get an idea of what strategies and processes can help them meet their goals. At this stage, Launch is working more as a business coach, giving them strategic advice along the way while we listen to their needs, desires, and vision.

This part of the process was adapted from the Strategic Coach® Program and a concept which its founder, Dan Sullivan, refers to as the D.O.S.

Conversation® reviewing the dangers, opportunities, and strengths of the clients.

Let's face it—when you're starting a real estate project, your mind goes into overdrive. But, at Launch, we have checklists and procedures we follow to ensure we don't miss anything.

We like to start with this scenario. Imagine you and I are meeting three years from today, and looking back over those three years, what needs to happen for you to feel like you've made progress on your development? We pay attention to what you say and look for clues that tell us what direction you want to go and the biggest issues surrounding your development that we need to assist in solving. Without this information, we're ill-equipped to help you flesh out your vision.

These are some of the things that get discussed in this part of the conversation:

- annexation issues

- obtaining entitlements for the project

- negotiating a development agreement with the jurisdiction

- expected or actual conditions of approval

- off-site and on-site infrastructure requirements and construction phasing

- oversizing of facilities

- cost sharing agreements

- other benefiting landowners
- provision of water/sewer / dry utilities
- types of financing available
- development impact fees
- development impact fee credits
- economic conditions
- home builder/home buyer lot preferences
- amenities
- federal/state permitting process. . . and much more.

Once this conversation has ended, we have a much deeper understanding of where we're going and can dive into more specific questions that continue to guide us throughout the project.

Two Options. One Choice.

The next step encompasses what we call the Launch Sequence™, which dives into planning, implementation, and management of your project financing. Right now, we want to focus on the steps we take during the planning phase of the Launch Sequence or what we refer to as the Path & Plan™ because the choices we make here will inform the steps we take along the way, as well as our client's future success.

The first step in the planning process starts with the concept that our clients have two options and one choice. We begin by asking, "From a financial perspective, are you internal rate of return (IRR) driven or nominal dollar driven (NDD)?"

IRR essentially means you want or need your money to come back to you as quickly as possible. This is ideal for clients whose revenue needs are more short-term. Typically, we see developers IRR driven if they have involved high-priced private equity in their project or if they're a publicly traded company (e.g., public home building company). In this scenario, you understand you generate more money over time, but you're willing to forgo that larger revenue stream to receive the money quicker.

In contrast, if you're not concerned about how long it takes to return your money, you might choose an NDD strategy. Because, at the end of the day, your primary goal is to maximize the total dollars returned to you regardless of the time these funds are received. Whether this takes fifteen or thirty years is of no consequence—you just want that bigger number. Now, these projects often terminate in ten or twenty years, so an NDD strategy is fairly common.

But what if you want to combine both strategies? With the way these projects work, going after both IRR and NDD isn't possible because they represent two completely different financing paths. We will do our best to try and accommodate your plan; however, we need a primary driving strategy to build your Path & Plan. Both strategies have pros and cons to them—you simply have to decide what strategy works best for you and your project.

Then, once you make this decision, Launch has a better idea of what road we're going to travel to help you reach your destination.

Just the Facts, Ma'am.

When you're talking about starting a large project, you must understand what the project's existing property taxes are. With the Land to Lots™ strategies, we walk our clients through layering on another ad valorem tax or special assessment payment, which will increase their property taxes as a result. For us to do that, we need to know where the property is currently located and where the project may be annexed anytime in the future into an incorporated city or town.

This is where we dive deep into a project's current and future property tax rates. If the project is located within the county and you have to annex into the city for utility services, we need to understand what your property taxes will be once the annexation is completed.

We then need to understand the property taxes of your current and/or future competition. This is important because we don't want to increase our total effective property tax burden to such a level that you can't sell lots to home builders or homes to home buyers. When reviewing the competitive market, we make objective and subjective decisions related to your project's strengths vis-a-vis the competition. Depending on where we are on this scale, we may either want to match the competition's tax rates or raise them a little higher than the competition if your project is at a competitive advantage.

With this property tax rate differential, we can estimate how much money we can issue over time with bonds that will finance the public infrastructure you plan to build for that area. During this phase of the analysis, we also keep in mind that our clients are in the business of selling lots and/or homes and not doing special district financings. We have to be sure that our clients will be able to deliver a quality product with a reasonable property tax burden.

The Art and the Science.

There is both an art and a science to determining whether we will max the current property taxes or if we will go slightly over the current rate. This is a concept called market acceptance. In other words, does the market want or need what you're offering and would they be willing to pay more property taxes to have what you're offering?

One scenario might be that the area has an influx of people moving into the city, yet they don't have enough residential neighborhoods to accommodate that demand. In a case like that, you'd be proving market acceptance right off the bat. The demand is there—as long as you're offering something comparable. In this instance, it's the law of supply and demand, and given the lack of supply (at least, in the short term), the buyers don't have a choice.

Under another scenario, there are multiple competitive projects in the area from which the buyers have a high degree of discretion. In this instance, and to the extent that because you have increased your total effective property tax burden as a result of the district, and to the extent that your property tax rate is higher than the competition, you will want to be able to point to items that make your community more desirable than the others. For example, you could show the prospective buyers you have used district proceeds to accelerate the construction of major roadways or schools, added enhanced landscaping to rights-of-way, or funded a large park, open spaces, and trails for the residents. In this way, the prospective buyers can make a buying decision related to whether they believe they are receiving ample value for the additional property tax payment.

It's also important to remember that real estate will change over time and that you have allowed for this in your various development and financing agreements. In this stage, we're starting to formulate how we might address the issues of flexibility for your unique project.

We start asking questions like these:

- What infrastructure are we required to build and what is its estimated cost?

- When are we required to build these facilities?

- What is the least amount of infrastructure we need to turn on the first tap or flush the first toilet?

- Can the jurisdiction fund any of these improvements?

- What kind of district financings are available?

- What is the timing and amount of potential district financing options?

- Can we ask the jurisdiction for sales tax and/or property tax increment?

- Who else benefits from these improvements?

- Does the jurisdiction use impact fees, system development fees, or other reimbursement mechanisms?

- How close can we get to financing as much of the infrastructure as possible?

- Etcetera, etcetera, etcetera.

Once we have the answers, we begin to assemble all the puzzle pieces allowing us to begin to handcraft a custom-crafted Path & Plan to help you provide flexibility for future changes in the economy and move you toward the vision you articulated in the D.O.S. Conversation®.

City within a City

Normally, when a developer makes plans to develop a master-planned community or other large project, there are zoning restrictions that dictate how the land can be used and what infrastructure can be built. But there are cities that have limited to no zoning restrictions (e.g., Houston, TX), giving you an open door to develop the type of community you envision without worrying about rigid jurisdictional restrictions.

We've worked with developers who build large master-planned communities that range in size from anywhere from 1,000 to 56,000 acres. You're essentially building a city within a city as your residents will live, work, and play in these master planned communities. These are highly planned communities where it goes beyond just developing neighborhoods. You might build schools, parks, recreational amenities, town centers, commercial centers, libraries, police and fire facilities, and other civic uses. You're only limited by your imagination—and, of course, by what the builders and/or home buyers want.

This is where it gets into privatization. Though all this infrastructure is available to the public, it's the private sector coming together to make these incredible spaces possible for the community. You're giving kids a safe place to ride their bikes, areas where moms can meet other moms for brunch, and meeting spaces where businesses can start, grow, and develop their visions. If you're dealing with a family-centric community, you want the children in the community to go from elementary school to junior high to high school all within the confines of your "city within a city."

You're not building the jurisdiction's vision for what they want their community to grow into—you're building *your* vision of the dream community that the market wants.

One of the areas with the greatest amount of zoning freedom is Houston, Texas, which has some of the top master-planned communities in the United States. Houston has no zoning restrictions, so we've been able to help real estate developers there buildtop-selling master-planned communities that we want to withstand the test of time. As some of these projects will be built out over twenty to fifty years, who knows what will happen in that amount of time?

This is why the art and the science of building in flexibility with financing is so integral to these projects.

Master Plan Insurance Policy.

These master-planned communities become insurance policies because they're providing more value than standard residential subdivisions. Homeowners and business owners coming into these communities may question why they're asked to pay more in property taxes than other non-master-planned communities without districts. Your answer to those concerns is based on all the value you're adding to the community:

- integrated master development plan

- mix of land uses all within proximity to residents

- town centers

- enhanced public infrastructure

- highly "amenitized" recreational facilities (parks, trails, open space, golf courses, community centers)

- quality-controlled architectural standards

- safe and secure neighborhoods

- integrated social and cultural enrichment programs

- multiple educational offers (public schools, charter schools)

- public safety facilities

- ... and much, much more

The infrastructure and facilities you build in the first phase of your community need to set the stage for prospective homeowners and business owners so they see the value in the additional property tax they're being asked to pay for the privilege of living, working, and playing in your development. You're building into your plan things that will always be valuable to your residents, whether the market is good or bad.

In our experience, given all the attributes of the master-planned community enumerated above, the values of residential homes increase faster in good times and hold their value more in down markets than do residential homes located in non-master-planned communities. This represents the built-in insurance policy you will provide your project's residents.

2

Presenting the Plan

This book isn't comprehensive of our entire Path & Plan process, but I hope that it gives you enough information to start thinking critically about our Land to Lots strategies. But, for those who want a bit more detail about how we get from the planning stages to the strategy that helps us complete the process, I'd like to go over our Project Diagnostic Review™ to help you dive a bit deeper.

The Project Diagnostic Review is a complicated in-depth surgical process that helps us ensure we're capturing all the revenue possibilities for the project. There will be some math involved in this step if you want to get into the weeds, but that's not necessary.

We start with a review of your community's

- land use plan

- development agreement (if available)

- construction costs

- project pro forma

The first area that we're going to look at is special purpose taxing districts. So, we want to know whether you've included the use of special-purpose taxing districts. And don't worry if you've never worked with these districts before because that's what we specialize in—this is exactly what I mean when I say it's possible to borrow money without having to pay it back. I've already laid out this strategy, so we won't dive into it here. But at this point, I'll ask why you haven't considered using them yet. If this is something you haven't looked at, we like to analyze why you're leaving money on the table.

If it's not in your plan, we will highly recommend you add that in because it makes your development even more attractive than your competitor's because you're creating a better mousetrap. These special-purpose taxing districts can help offset some of those costs, lower your overall cost of capital, and enhance your revenues.

We then move into a review of your construction costs and when you anticipate these funds to be expended. We are trying to understand what infrastructure has to be built when and what the jurisdiction's expectations are as to what the scope of the infrastructure will be. We do this deep dive into the numbers because we're performing what we call the RED Analysis™, reduce, eliminate, and defer. As the IRR will be largely influenced by the amount of funds expended in the early years of the project, we are attempting to do our best to reduce, eliminate, or defer these costs until later in the development process when you can begin recognizing revenue events.

An example of reducing, eliminating, or deferring costs is best illustrated by a recent project we worked on in the Southwest. In this particular instance, the municipality wanted our client to build a four-lane divided arterial road as part of the project's first phase of development. Working with the municipal staff, we were able to convince them to allow our client to only construct two of the four lanes until the 500th building permit was pulled. In this way, we were able to push these costs out for approximately five years during a period when our client would be receiving revenues from the sale of super pads to home builders.

Oftentimes, especially in California, jurisdictions tell us that because residential development does not pay for itself (something I have found NOT to be true), the jurisdiction wants our client to provide some amount of capital to their general fund to help offset the operational costs they will incur. When this occurs, we ask the municipality to show us their math on how they arrived at this figure. Nine times out of ten, they can't provide an analysis. If they do provide the analysis, we will review their assumptions and results and compare those assumptions with the costs of services derived from the municipality's Comprehensive Annual Financial Report (CAFR). In our experience, the municipality's assumptions are not congruent with actual costs as outlined in the CAFR, and we can reduce or fully eliminate the requested subsidy amount.

The third thing we do is focus on the development impact fees (DIF) and DIF credit analysis. We can take this conversation one of two ways. Land developer clients like to see DIFs, especially as they relate to their project, as large as possible. They like to see that they have that money coming back to repay them for the large regional infrastructure they're building. However, on the home builder side, they like to see the DIFs as low as possible. We are caught in the middle and believe that DIF are a necessary evil, as long as they're fair and equitable to all parties involved.

If we have a line item in the pro forma related to DIF, we look at the purpose of the impact fees. There's a lot of case law behind DIFs as well as industry standards. This is where we deal with the whole concept of the dual rational nexus test, which means there has to be a nexus, or a cause, for an individual developer or builder to pay the impact fee. And that impact fee has to be proportional to the financial impact caused by the demand for new services, roads, water, sewer, etc. With the case law and industry standards along with over thirty decades of reviewing DIF studies for our private sector clients, we can easily drill down to determine if the DIFs are reasonable and consistent with the dual rational nexus test and case law.

At Launch, we have worked a lot for the National Association of Homebuilders and various builder industry associations around the country to evaluate the reasonableness of impact fees and to fight those fees when appropriate. To date, we've averaged a 24.6 percent reduction of DIFs, because many times, DIFs are made as instructed by the municipality, and their consultants (some, not all) will cook the books and magically end up with the DIF requested by the municipality.

If that amount is not fair or equitable, we're going to fight it and ask for a reduction in the DIF amount. This step ensures we're adhering to case law, industry standards, and the concept of dual rational nexus test. On the other hand, if we're building a very large master-planned community that will benefit the entire community, we'll ask the city to reimburse the developer for the infrastructure through an impact fee based on supportable cost and levels of service analysis.

Once we have determined the DIFs are reasonable, we then want to find the amount of funding coming back to the master developer in terms of DIF reimbursements or DIF credits. It is necessary to ensure the repayment of the DIFs is documented and the methodology for their calculation is clearly outlined in the development agreement to avoid misinterpretation by future municipal staff members.

There are also other infrastructure cost-reduction strategies, which is why we ask about other benefitting landowners or developers nearby. If you're required to build a lot of infrastructure to develop that land, it isn't fair to you if you're the only one investing in building up the area. The nearby developers and landowners are riding on your coattails. Why would they want to pay for it if someone else is already committed to doing so? We'll want to work with the jurisdiction and make sure the other developers and landowners also pay their fair share of that infrastructure. Most of the time, jurisdictions will agree and create an ordinance that requires the other developers to fund their pro-rata share of the costs of the infrastructure. We call this establishing a Reimbursement Mechanism, and we have multiple strategies to make other benefiting landowners pay for their share of the infrastructure costs sooner rather than later.

Question Everything

It's our job to go through the land use plan, development agreement (if available), construction costs, and pro forma and question everything. Once we've done our analysis, we outline multiple financing scenarios to help the clients achieve their business plan. We meet with them, explain the pros and cons of each scenario, allow them to ask questions, and make the final decision concerning what financing scenario works best for them.

After we explain what the available strategies are for this particular client, we lay out the pros and cons of each. We like to equip our clients with the right information that empowers them to make intelligent decisions about their business or their project.

To contrast, let's talk about how other consultants might handle a similar project. Once they meet with a potential client, regardless of the client's goals, they propose only one solution, the one solution most advantageous to the consultant. To them, regardless of what the client is trying to achieve, they only view the client's challenges as a nail, and they only offer "their hammer" as the solution. I've found that to prepare our clients—all our clients, not only one type of client—for success, we need an array of financial tools on our toolbelt. We come prepared with different sizes of hammers, screwdrivers, levels, saws, etc. This opens up a lot of possibilities and opportunities those clients might not be aware of when they're working with a consultant who sees the problem only as a nail.

One size does not fit all, so we like to provide our clients with an array of financial possibilities that allow them to get to where they want to go as quickly and as efficiently as possible. We want to open our client's eyes to multiple possibilities and have them question everything.

There is an old saying, "It ain't what you don't know that gets you into trouble. It's what you know for sure that just ain't so."

So, even if you think you're certain of something, I still think it's important to question that knowledge. Keep asking yourself questions like this: "Why do I have to do it that way?" In the pursuit of success, you can't always find it by following the breadcrumbs others have left behind. In some cases, you will want to, of course, follow others' advice and techniques. However, you should always ask questions so you have the reassurance that it's the right path for you and your business.

Toyota Industries Founder Sakichi Toyoda developed his "Five Whys" technique that makes great use of why it's important to question everything. Here is the process Toyoda defined back in the 1930s, adjusted a bit for our "question everything" philosophy:[1]

1. Assemble your team to help solve the problem (answer the question) at hand.

2. Define the problem (or answer the question) you're currently facing.

3. Ask the first "Why?"

4. Ask "Why?" four more times to dig deeper to uncover a more-focused answer or solution.

5. Realize the point where you should stop asking questions—know when enough is enough.

6. Address the root cause or concern that caused you to "question everything" to begin with.

7. Determine whether you've addressed your initial concern.

[1] Mind Tools Content Team. "5 Whys—Problem-Solving Skills From MindTools.com." Mind Tools. Accessed October 24, 2022. https://www.mindtools.com/pages/article/newTMC_5W.htm.

Memorialize the Decision

Once we lay out the various solutions for our clients, meet them to discuss the pros and cons of the various financing scenarios, and they have selected the best solution, we then memorize their Path & Plan in a three- to four-page write-up with location maps, land use plans, cost estimates, and high-level financing summaries, which we call the Finance Plan™. The purpose of the Finance Plan is to outline the client's preferred Path & Plan for presentation to the jurisdiction to solicit their input and approval of the high-level concepts outlined in the Finance Plan. This is an important step in the financing process because we don't want to spend a lot of time and our client's money trying to establish financing if the jurisdiction is not going to approve and support it.

Present at a High Level

We prepare and present the Finance Plan at such a high level because we want all parties to be prepared for what's to come. At this stage, we check what the jurisdiction will agree to and if it aligns with our client's goals. We want to know of any potential issues that might come down the pipeline. If we don't detect any issues at this point, we typically have a green light to move forward with the financing outlined in the Finance Plan. However, many projects won't be this straightforward. These projects can often be complex, so there might be some challenges to work through at this point.

Keeping that in mind, though, a green light now doesn't mean there won't be any obstacles further down the road. Most projects have some sort of challenge that needs to be addressed during some stage of the process. We're accustomed to working with many different types of obstacles and can tackle those challenges with the wide array of financing tools we have in our toolbelt.

District Financing and Development Agreements

Establishing a district when a project development exists can be tricky. In multiple instances, we have found that jurisdictions may try to renegotiate an existing development agreement as part of the establishment of the district. For instance, in one of our transactions in which a development agreement existed, the developer had agreed to build and equip a fire station once 500 building permits had been issued. As part of the district negotiations, the jurisdiction stipulated that for them to support the establishment of the district, the developer would have to build the fire station in conjunction with the development of the first phase of development. The economics of this project were such that the developer agreed to their request. However, we generally try to avoid this situation by including district financing agreements as an exhibit to the development agreement as it is being initially negotiated, or we establish the district at the same meeting the development agreement is approved. That way, we can't be "held up" by the jurisdiction when we ask to establish the district.

It's important to note that the professionals at Launch work only with the private sector, so we're quite clear on where our loyalties lie. Some consultants who make these deals work in both the public and the private sectors. Whether I'm making multiple deals in that jurisdiction, I handle each transaction as if it were our only deal with that jurisdiction. We work this way because we want all our clients to understand that we do not make cookie-cutter deals—every project financing we work on is custom-crafted to that client's goals and objectives.

One of our leading principles at Launch is that every deal is different, and we stand by that promise.

The Client Counts

The client and their vision is the most important factor in the work we do. In some instances, we have seen clients work exclusively with underwriters to establish districts and issue bonds. While we work closely with the underwriting community, the challenge with underwriters structuring transactions is that most of them specialize in one type of transaction. They do this because it's the easiest for the underwriter. It's important to remember that underwriters don't work for developers—they work for the bondholders. Launch professionals, however, work exclusively for the developers.

Because of that, if one underwriting firm can't structure the deal the way our client wants, we find another underwriter who is more than happy to structure the transaction—the right way being the exact way our client needs it to be executed. All clients and projects have a different D.O.S., and this is exactly why every one of our deals is custom-made to our client's needs.

What works for one developer is not always going to work for another developer, and this is one of the most important foundations we've built our strategies on.

PART 2

Implementing the Finance Plan

3

Creating the Money

Create Certainty

At this point, this is where the real work starts as we begin to execute the project financing. We've got our client's D.O.S., the Finance Plan, and the jurisdiction's input. With all this information, we've collectively decided we're going to move forward with the Finance Plan. The next thing we do is create the legal documents that cover everything we've decided up until this point.

Now, I'm not an attorney, but I've drafted a lot of legal documents as they relate to my expertise—finance. In these legal documents, I want to create certainty and flexibility. Certainty is important for us and our clients because key members in the jurisdiction's staff will come and go—city council members, city managers, city attorneys, and so on. However, the project we're working on will be a part of this jurisdiction for many years, and we don't want new staff members second-guessing our Finance Plan and trying to change it. For this reason, we must include in the legal agreements including, but not limited to, the development agreement and district financing agreements, clear unambiguous language related to who's doing what and when. This level of clarification is critical to avoid new staff members, who may be trying to make a name for themselves, from misinterpreting and renegotiating the documents later.

Create Flexibility

We're certain the market will change multiple times over the development of the project, and buyers' preferences will also change over time. For this reason, we want to memorialize within the agreement's multiple options for the developer, so that as the market changes, the developer can adjust to those changes without having to amend existing jurisdictional or district financing agreements.

Examples of creating flexibility include allowing densities to move so long as developers are not exceeding the overall agreed-to total amount of allowable units. Flexibility also might mean allowing districts to finance any type of public facilities allowed by law as opposed to specific infrastructure. We have hundreds of ways to create flexibility, but remember that you want to create sufficient flexibility in your documents so that when the economy changes or when you may need to address specific changes to your development program, you don't have to go back to the jurisdiction or district to amend your agreements. If you do, it will cost you money. In our experience, the jurisdictions or districts will be willing to amend your agreement. However, they more than likely want something in return. This is the discussion you are trying to avoid, and you avoid this discussion by creating flexibility upfront in the agreement.

Development Agreement

There are two situations I run into when I'm working on this document—either the developer needs to annex into a city because they need utilities, or the developers are already annexed into the jurisdiction. Each scenario requires a development agreement.

One agreement is the pre-annexation development agreement (PADA). A PADA covers when the real estate developer needs to come into the city and they need to craft a deal regarding the city's various requirements. The development agreement is drawn up when the real estate is already annexed. This memorializes our client's understanding with the city related to many of the same issues included in the PADA. It outlines what the client will do for this current project and what the city will provide.

These PADA agreements dive deep into land use issues, total allowed units, utility provision, required infrastructure, the timing of construction, schools, public safety, and financing. When we develop the PADA, we like to put in specific yet easy-to-understand language that creates certainty and flexibility for our clients and can easily be understood by elected officials and staff, and limits the number of attorneys reading the document.

Will vs. May

Many times, the jurisdiction will include language in the development agreement that the jurisdiction "may consider the use of a special purpose taxing district." We object to this language as our client is agreeing to annex into the jurisdiction or is committing to spending tens of millions of dollars for public infrastructure, and we need to know for sure that the jurisdiction "will" create a special taxing district.

In one instance, our client was in a hurry to secure their zoning entitlements, and they agreed to the "may" language, believing the jurisdiction would live up to their word to establish the district. However, when the developer asked them to establish the district, the city indicated they would if the developer agreed to build and equip a fire station and pay one million dollars per year for ten years to staff the fire station. Essentially, the city blackmailed them. We want to avoid this from happening in the future with our development agreements.

And that's the power of words—"will" versus "may." On the surface, it seems like such a tiny difference, but in these agreements, a word can make or break a deal.

In more complex financings, we will create exhibits within the agreement that outline how calculations will be performed and where the data to complete the financing calculations come from. That way, both parties know what to expect—there are no surprises or blindsides down the road.

In the blackmailing situation, our client had to take the lumps and do what the jurisdiction asked. The $15 million we were going to use for other facilities went toward the fire station. Our client had to pay out of pocket for that expense, then they had to fund the $1 million for the fire station operations for ten years. It was a huge mistake that cost the client a lot of money, and we tell our future clients this story as a warning against doing things too quickly and the difference between "will" and "may."

I tell the client, "This has happened to me once, but it will never happen again." Although, this circumstance wasn't a result of something Launch did—it was the client who ultimately made the decision—we vowed never to create a situation where it would happen to another client in the future. Because, as I mentioned earlier in this book, we are only as good as our last transaction. This was a huge learning experience for everyone involved.

The Power of the Checklist

That blackmail situation became a part of our Project Financing Checklist™. This is a running document we keep of hard lessons learned and things we could have been done better. We track everything so ~~all~~ our next projects can be even more successful. This works well for me, so I am a firm believer in using this checklist. It's eight pages long and covers all the things we don't ever want to happen in a transaction. With every transaction we do, we run through this list to protect our clients and ourselves.

The Project Financing Checklist is chock-full of forty-plus years of learning experiences throughout my career as well as the wisdom of my clients. I believe in this checklist so much that I believe it's worth hundreds of millions of dollars. It's an integral part of our success that we bring to the Launch Sequence and all our client's financing structures.

Control the District

Control of the district is an important aspect of our deals, possibly the key to the entire transaction. For example, some state-enabling statutes provide developers with much more control of the district governance, which is ideal for our situation. When the developer is in control, they have more certainty that bonds will be issued and when they will be issued than if the jurisdiction controls the governance of the district. States that have favorable financing statutes: Arizona (Revitalization District), Colorado (Metropolitan District), Florida (Community Development District), and Texas (Municipal Utility District and the Municipal Management District).

If we don't have that certainty, we must request that the jurisdictional control district board issue bonds to finance eligible public infrastructure. While this is not the end of the world, it does mean that more time, effort, and costs will be incurred to withdraw money from the ATM we've attached to our project (e.g., the district) and that our ATM fee has gone from $5 to $100.

Additionally, the jurisdictional board could decide they're not going to issue any more bonds in your district. And they can do this legally because we can't force a district into making a legislative finding or an action. However, if we're in control of the district, we know that never will happen because we're the decision-makers.

Let's look at the infrastructure listing, or what you might call the shopping basket of costs that we can fund with districts. Usually, we can only finance public infrastructures, which are those facilities owned and operated by counties, cities, towns or districts. But we can add other infrastructures to the shopping basket, if we are forward-thinking, such as real property, rights-of-way, police and fire station sites, public park sites, trails, and open spaces.

We can also turn once-private infrastructure into public infrastructure. For instance, oftentimes the district cannot finance private recreational centers.

However, what we can do is open the recreational center to the public, allow all homeowners within the community to come and go without charge, and charge the non-community residents a daily use fee. As most people will not be willing to pay the daily use fee, rarely will you have to concern yourself with outside users, but now we can finance the community center through the district because it is a "public" amenity. Having a larger shopping list gives you much more that you can finance. It also allows us to pick and choose what items we want to finance through the district so we can accelerate cash into the pro forma or have a larger shopping basket to fund over time. And, when you have those things, the largest nominal dollars are being paid to you over time by the district.

For instance, on one of our transactions, the eligible public infrastructure costs were $525 million. However, over the estimated fifty-year build-out of the project, the potential bonding capacity of this district was $1.3 billion, but I didn't have that much in eligible costs. So, in the district financing agreements. I wrote in that the district would repay the developer the financing costs that accrued when they advanced the funds for the cost of the infrastructure.

Einstein supposedly said, "The most powerful force in the universe is compound interest." At Launch, we took that concept to move our eligible reimbursable costs from $525 million to $1.3 billion, where approximately $775 million of that was financing costs. Now, whether we get all that money remains to be seen, but that's the idea behind creating the larger shopping basket.

Different districts can issue different bond types; however, there are three types of bonds used in special-purpose taxing districts: revenue bonds, general obligation bonds, and assessment bonds. So, depending upon the state we are working in, we want to use all eligible bond types so we can pick and choose what kind of bonds we use. We want to set the bond authorization to be a high number, so we never run out of money at our ATM and never have to hold another bond authorization election.

In other words, when we set up the districts, the developer typically has one election to authorize our cost of, for example, $100 million. I recommend we don't set up the district for $100 million; rather, we set up the district for $250 million to account for cost inflation, home price appreciation, real property interests, and potentially financing costs. After the election, I don't want to tell the residents we screwed-up the bond election for $100 million. That would require us to come back and say, "Now that you're living here, would you mind voting yes, so I can tax you an extra $150 million?" That's not an accessible conversation with residents, which is why we do it upfront when we're the only voter.

The new homeowners buying the homes in this developer's district are aware of this bond election, and they sign off on it when they agree to purchase their home. It doesn't seem like an issue to them at the time because they're also getting into these great school districts, golf courses, beautiful homes, etc., so they don't think the extra taxes are a big deal. It's the cost they're willing to pay for living in this premium master-planned community. We do our due diligence and tell them what their property tax is, and they acknowledge their responsibility to pay that. However, most people stay in a house for less than ten years, so the property taxes, they figure, will be somebody else's responsibility after they move to their next home. At the moment of purchase, they're deciding whether they can afford the monthly mortgage. What's not important to them is how much of the payment goes to principal, interest, and taxes. They're not tasked with doing the math.

We want to be able to set the tax rates so the scales tip in our favor. That gives us the ability to raise the bond, even though we may not need that. In the worst-case scenario, we're establishing a floor we can live with that we determined during our Path & Plan process. I create that flexibility so I can raise the amount if necessary, but I know for certain I won't go below my floor as it relates to all the items we discussed related to flexibility.

Keep in mind, too, that it's rare to see a case of underspending because infrastructure costs are always increasing. That's one reason why flexibility is so important. I want my clients to have a lot of choices, and that's what we're trying to set up with this strategy.

With one of our clients, we set up a bond authorization of $1.3 billion. I told my client I couldn't ask for a billion dollars, but remember what I said about questioning everything? We did some financial analysis on this figure and proved that we could support the $1.3 billion figure, and the city agreed. That blew us away, and we wondered if we could have asked for $1.6 billion.

Some people will look at that number and say that's a big number. Some of the bondholders felt it would hurt us when we were issuing bonds. But that was just their opinion, which wasn't backed by any facts or figures. Now, we have facts to support this ask. We haven't had any problems selling bonds with that $1.3 billion authorization.

And this number helps us create flexibility for our clients.

PART 3

Managing the Finance Plan

4

Withdrawing the Money

Check the Boxes

One of our mantras is to help our clients finance infrastructure, reduce their costs, and mitigate their risks. To handle the risk side, we have developed great tools and unique processes to help our clients achieve these goals. For instance, the industry standard related to the use of special assessment bonds is to borrow 33 percent of the assessed property's fair market value, but if warranted, we will work with the underwriters and seek the bond buyers' approval to borrow 50 percent of the fair market value instead. We know they will charge us a higher interest rate for the added risk they are taking on. We then leave the decision of whether this is a cost they care to bear to the developer. Most times, they will because the cost of borrowing 17 percent more money at a tax-exempt interest is much cheaper than the cost of equity.

When we work on reducing costs, we do a RED Analysis™, which stands for reduce, eliminate, and defer. For example, as part of the development agreement, the city might want our client to build a four-lane, divided arterial road. Not only that, but they need it to have a landscaped median, left turn lanes, and signal lights. The city wants this road on day one.

We negotiate with the city because we know the road will handle much more traffic than projected initially. We agree to the four-lane road, but we want to make a little adjustment—we offer to build only two lanes to start. A tactic like this allows us to reduce the amount of capital we need at the beginning of the project. In theory, those other two lanes can wait until we absolutely need them, or after we have constructed a specific number of homes built within the community with certificates of occupancy.

This strategy removes a lot of the upfront burden from the developer because it takes a huge amount of money to sell that first lot. So, in that example, we want to push off non-essential infrastructure because we don't yet have the tax base or land value to fund non-essential infrastructure. This gives both parties a bit of what they want and need to get the project started and allows us to defer these costs further in the project's pro forma when we are generating cash from sales of lots to builders and thereby enhancing our project's IRR.

Track the Costs

One other thing that's going to come into play is the responsibility that comes with using public money to fund public infrastructure. Funding projects this way requires the developer to retain and assemble a lot of documentation because the public must know we spent the money for its intended purposes—the roads, water, sewer, public parks, etc. So, when the developers ask to be repaid for such costs, they must provide third-party evidence that they followed all the state's and district's public procurement protocols. Depending on the state, this information can include notices inviting bids, public notices of bid posting, pre-bid meeting notes, bid packages, certification of bids, award of bids, contracts, draw requests, change orders, canceled checks, certified payrolls, lien waivers, and acceptance of infrastructure letters by the jurisdiction.

All that information must go somewhere, so if our clients aren't equipped to handle this record-keeping challenge, we have our Launch Reimbursement System™ (LRS) that manages that process for them. The LRS is one of the unique processes we've developed, a huge electronic database that houses this information. So, when it comes time to submit the reimbursement request, we hit a button to start the process, and the LRS puts everything together, summarizes it, and sends it to the city or district so we can get the money to reimburse our clients.

Read the Rules

Financing projects with districts comes with a lot of rules you must follow, and we're here to help our clients so they understand these rules. These clients are land developers, industrial developers, mixed-use developers, and home builders, not special district experts. Our clients simply want to know everything they don't have their hands in is still taken care of, and we manage that for them so all they must do is be notified of when the check will be in the mailbox.

Don't Lose the ATM Card

When we're talking about financing these development projects through the bonds we issue, we need a way to access that financing. This is what we call the ATM. Because we're managing the access to those funds, we're making sure it's constantly filled with money so our clients have the financing to build out their project.

If we're going to create the ATM, it does nobody any good if individuals in the organization don't know anything about the ATM. They often don't know how you turn the thing on—they're always relying on somebody else to have this knowledge. So, they need to designate someone to hold onto this ATM card—either a long-term staff member or Launch can hold onto it for them. We've been here for over forty years—we're not going anywhere. Clients know they can rely on us to keep track of the card.

Use the Card

At the end of the day, all our clients want is for us to "show them the money", to borrow a phrase from *Jerry Maguire*. So, we use these systems to manage and report out to our clients. Sometimes, we meet with the public builders weekly because they are managing their cash flows to report to Wall Street and want to hit their earnings and free cash flow goals. These builders want their money sooner rather than later, so we use these tools along with the LRS to accelerate cash and make sure everybody on the homebuilding team is doing what they need to give us the information. We're not necessarily writing the checks or preparing the contracts—those things come from the developer. We arrange to meet weekly to ensure everyone is in the loop and communicating, so our clients have access to the funds they need for the project sooner rather than later.

PART 4

Countdown

5

Time to Launch

You're Still Reading for a Reason

Is this a dream you're still holding in your heart, or are you planning to launch your first Land to Lots project? If you're ready to take that first step, then our team at Launch is ready to walk alongside you.

You're still reading for a reason, and I'm willing to bet your reason is that these concepts resonate deeply with you. If you're ready to blast off with Launch, here are some of the states we recommend looking at for your first (or next) project:

- Arizona
- California

- Colorado

- Florida

- Idaho

- Nevada

- New Mexico

- Texas

- Utah

These are the states that have the best enabling statutes for these types of special district opportunities. Or maybe you want to dig in deeper and talk to us about setting up the right conditions in your state, even if the legislation isn't there to support such a project. If that's something you're interested in, we can help draft the legislation to get it passed. We do this with our Legislative Gameplan™, in which we work with developers to draft and lobby special district legislation. To date, we have drafted and passed legislation in Arizona, Idaho, New Mexico, Nevada, North Carolina, and Texas, and it can be done for other states. The plan for these types of projects looks much different, but I don't want you to feel like the opportunity is not there—it's simply a different road you must travel.

That brings us full circle back to what I talked about in the beginning—**every deal is different**. And, to go even further than that, every client we work with is different.

So, if you're ready, I'd love to start the conversation—I'd love to know where you want to go. If I can be your travel agent on this journey, I am more than happy to take that trip with you.

Self-Evaluation

Here are some questions you can ask yourself (and jot down some quick answers) to get started with the Land to Lots process:

1. What are the milestones that we must achieve over the next three years to ensure that the project is on track?

2. What thoughts pop up at 3:00 in the morning that may prevent may keep me from achieving the milestones outlined above?

3. What really excites me about this project?

4. What are my or my company's strong points as it relates to moving this project forward? What do I/we bring to the table to achieve the project's milestones?

Our team loves to help others talk through these questions. In fact, it's where all our conversations begin, focusing on our client's bigger future.

APPENDIX A

Land to Lots Case Studies

Here is a small sampling of special district financing transactions:

Floreo at Teravalis—This represents the first 3,000 acres of the larger 37,000-acre Teravalis master planned community located in the City of Buckeye, Arizona. The developer is currently in the planning phase of this project and is working with the City of Buckeye to establish multiple special districts to finance the hundreds of millions of public infrastructure.

Eastmark—This is a 2,170-acre project located in Mesa, Arizona. The developer established the community facilities district to issue both general obligation and special assessment bonds to finance the acquisition of public infrastructure over time as the development of the project moves forward. The CFD has established an ad valorem tax rate increase of $3.85 per $100 of assessed valuation and is also issuing assessment bonds of approximately $3,500 per lot.

Eastmark

Estancia Hill Country—Estancia Hill County is a 593-acre project located in the Lake Travis area of Austin, Texas. The developer established a public improvement district to fund the construction and/or acquisition of water, sewer, drainage, roadways, landscaping, and trails.

Village of Sendero—This represents approximately a 416-acre project in Orange County, California, in which the developer issued CFD special tax bonds to finance public improvements.

Sienna Plantation—This 944-acre project located in Fort Bend, Texas, established a municipal utility district to issue general obligation bonds to acquire water, sewer, and drainage improvements.

Sienna Plantation

Summerlin—The developer established multiple special improvement districts over this approximate 22,500-acre development located in Clark County and Las Vegas, Nevada, to fund roadways, water, sewer, and drainage improvements.

Union Park—The developer of this 580-acre project located in Pasco County, Florida, established a community development district (CDD) to issue bonds to construct and/or acquire water, sewer, roadway, landscaping, and trail improvements.

APPENDIX B

Frequently Asked Questions

Question 1: What Can I Finance?

No matter what state we're working in, any infrastructure that will be owned and operated by a public entity. So, the keyword here is "public"—it's got to be owned by a city, a county, a town, or a quasi-political subdivision. The public infrastructure in these categories includes public roads, public water, public sewer, public storm drain, public parks, libraries, schools, fire stations, police stations, traffic lights, streetlights—any infrastructure that you would need to build a community, as long as it's public.

The next kind of subset is clients who have to build public infrastructure, but also may include a private guard gated community. They ask, "How will the guard gate impact my ability to finance infrastructure through the special purpose taxing district?" We could finance the roadway to the guard gate, and on the side of the guard gate that is private, we would not be able to finance the roads with public bonds. If, for instance, in the same example, we have public water and sewer lines run from the arterial road into the private guard gated community and under the private road, we could finance the public water and sewer facilities, both from the arterial roadway into the guard gate, and then into the community itself, because those water and sewer lines are owned and operated by, in this example, the city. Even though they're under a private road, we would be able to finance them through the district.

And I'm going to use the term district as a catch-all for all the different districts available around the United States. There are other kinds of cool nuances that we can do with infrastructure financing, depending upon what state we're in and what the specific statutes allow.

The concept is that if we're using public dollars to finance public infrastructure, the public has to be able to use it. So in the case of a roadway, that's pretty simple. When we're talking about amenity centers that may be constructed primarily for servicing the residents within a master-planned community, it becomes a little nuanced because the public has to be able to access that amenity center if we plan to finance the amenity center through public debt.

The issue we typically have with developers is that they don't want the public in their amenity centers—they want their amenity centers to be used exclusively by the residents. One of the ways that developers get around this problem is to have the district own and operate that amenity center. And that amenity center is open to all the residents of the master-planned community. Then the developers can demonstrate that there are residents of the community paying their HOA dues and as such, they can use that facility without any problems.

Now, if an individual from outside of the community comes in and wants to utilize that facility, they have to be allowed to use that facility. However, we can charge them a daily usage fee, which may be $75 per day, which is perfectly legal. And, as a result of that, you typically don't get public outside of the boundaries of the district or the master-planned coming in to use those facilities. However, because this strategy allows the recreation center to be public, we can finance it through the district.

Question 2: How Much Can I Borrow?

Everything is based, for the most part, on what type of bonds we will issue. More importantly, what is our tax rate compared to the competition's tax rate? The most important concept that I want to emphasize is we do not want to increase our project's property tax rate to a level where we make our project uncompetitive with the surrounding marketplace.

We will sit down with you, analyze your property tax bills, and prepare a list of communities that you anticipate your project to be competing against. Let's say, for instance, we have a master-planned community in the state of Arizona. They have a tax rate of $12 per $100 of assessed value, and our competition has a tax rate of $16 per 100 of assessed valuation. We can take our tax rate and raise it from $12 to $16. Theoretically, this would not impact our ability to compete against the competitive projects in the area as all projects will be at a $16 tax rate.

What we have found is that people typically don't beat a path to our door because we have a lower property tax rate, especially when we're talking about residential development. Most homebuyers are not familiar with property taxes—they don't understand them as much as commercial users do. They understand they have to pay them, but they don't compare tax rates in your community against somebody else's. The one exception is California, where most homebuyers are pretty savvy given the cost of homes and the impact that property taxes have on their ability to qualify for a mortgage. In other states, people will purchase that home for reasons other than property taxes.

Question 3: What Kind of Bonds Should I Issue?

That will depend on what state we're in and whether you are IRR or nominal-dollar-driven. So, for instance, there are four different bond types that we typically see with special-purpose taxing districts:

1. general obligation bond

2. special assessment bond

3. revenue bond

4. special tax levy bond (e.g. California and Hawaii)

The general obligation bond is secured by an increase in the *ad valorem* property tax of property contained within the boundaries of a district. This is Latin for "according to value," and that's exactly what it means. This property has to be on the tax roll before you're capable of generating any type of tax revenue from it. You'll typically see this type of bond in Texas, Arizona, and Colorado. (The only exception to this rule is that Colorado allows you to issue bonds upfront based on the anticipated value of the home rather than the actual value of the property contained within the district when the bonds are issued.)

The next bond type is a special assessment bond, which is secured by a specific lien on a specific piece of property. Let's assume that we're developing phase one of a two-phase project. We're issuing phase one's special assessment bond upfront, and we plan to use bond proceeds to construct public infrastructure specifically benefiting phase one. In this example, we'll assume we're building water, sewer, and roads that will front each lot. We secure the bonds with an assessment against each lot. For instance, if we issue $10 million in bonds and there are 600 lots in phase one, each lot will get an assessment of $16,666 ($10,000,000 /

600 lots) per lot. The bonds are issued, and the streets, roads, water, and sewer are constructed.

Assessment bonds are sized based on the fair market value of the land, assuming that the infrastructure to be financed through the bonds is in place as of the date of valuation. The beauty of the assessment bonds is it's a way for us to accelerate cash into the pro forma or use bond proceeds to build infrastructure benefiting that particular phase. And because we're using bond proceeds, we can reduce the amount of equity we're borrowing and thereby increase our IRR.

The third bond type is a revenue bond, though we don't see these bonds used much in big master-planned communities because we typically don't have a revenue source that can secure the issuance of such bonds. An example of a revenue stream could be a parking garage in the mixed-use project that generates daily parking revenue that you could quantify and use to secure epayment of a revenue bond.

One place where you see this done frequently is in Florida, where they might take an amenity fee charged by a master-planned developer for the residents to use amenities owned by the special district. They will often use the revenue generated by the amenity fee to support the revenue bonds used for the district to acquire the amenity center.

The special tax levy bond is primarily related to California and Hawaii and their community facilities districts (CFD). In this instance, a special tax levy is assessed on different categories of property and functions much like an assessment lien. Typically in California, we try not to push up total property taxes (including the CFD) as a percentage of home prices above 2 percent.

Question 4: What Are the Interest Rates of the Bonds?

The interest rate depends on how a developer can answer several questions. The answers the following questions will either make the risk increase to the buyer in which case the interest rate will rise, or they will make the risk decrease, in which case the interest will be reduced as the project is seen as a safer investment:

- What is the description of the project?
- Where is the project located?
- Is it located in a high-growth area?
- What is our current municipal interest rate environment?
- What are the mortgage rates?
- Does the developer have experience?
- What's the value of the land?
- How much money are we asking to borrow?
- Does the developer have "skin in the game"?
- What is the stage of this development?

- Do we have home builder contracts in hand from public or regional builders?

- Is this a brand-new development, or has it been around for a while?

- Does the developer have a good reputation?

- Is this the first bond issuance of the project?

- Is there anything we can do to credit enhance the bonds?

We need to be able to demonstrate that we have a great story or history behind this project so more investors will be interested in providing funding and thereby driving down interest rates on the bonds. To the extent that we can't generate a positive compelling story behind the project, the fewer investors and the higher the interest rate.

Question 5: What Are the Terms of the Bonds?

This is a pretty easy question. Typically, the terms of the bonds are twenty-five to thirty years, depending on the state where you're developing your community. Most transactions strive for the longest bond term because it allows us to issue the largest amount of bonds.

Question 6: Do I Have to Pay Off These Bonds When I Sell to a Builder or Homebuyer?

The short answer to that is no. But the idea behind issuing tax-exempt bonds is to pass that responsibility on to the end users of the project, and they will pay off those bonds over the terms set. If want the option to pay off bonds for whatever reason—typically, those are market driven—then we need to look at utilizing special assessment bonds and/or special tax levy bonds, where we can pre-pay the obligation in whole or in part.

Question 7: Who Buys These Bonds?

Our preference is to sell the bonds to institutions or institutional investors—meaning large bond funds, and/or institutions familiar with the ups and downs of real estate. These institutions typically have tons of experience buying bonds secured by land.

In the event that we have to do a workout, it is a lot easier to work with four or five men and women sitting around a conference table as opposed to 600 doctors and lawyers who don't understand the bond world. And, in the forty-plus years I've been doing this, I've been fortunate that none of the districts we have been involved in have ever gone south.

These bonds may also be sold to individuals— however, we shy away from that. We encourage our clients and underwriters to sell to institutions only. This is done by setting up denominations that are of such a size that only institutions are capable of purchasing them (e.g., $100,000 or greater).

Question 8: Will We Have to Reduce Home Prices with Special District Financing?

Because California is the exception, we're going to exclude it from the answer to this question. In our experience, it has not been necessary to reduce home prices. As long as we are setting our special district tax rate equivalent to the competition, we are not going to have to reduce our home price as a result of increasing our effective property taxes.

As a general rule, home buyers are not that sophisticated when it comes to property taxes. They know they have to pay them, but they don't compare rates or ask a lot of questions about them. At the end of the day, they're purchasing a monthly payment. Part of that monthly payment is the principal interest and property taxes. As long as they can afford that, they're happy. Their priority is to purchase a house they fell in love with at the model home complex, that is close to work, is in a good school district, or has great amenities—those are the most important things to home buyers.

Question 9: Do I Have to Pay Prevailing Wage?

In some states, you have to pay prevailing wage. In California and Nevada, when we're seeking reimbursement, we have to demonstrate that we have, in fact, paid a prevailing wage to all the contractors and their employees involved in the job. Now, in the other states—Florida, Texas, Colorado, Utah, Arizona, Idaho—we don't have to pay prevailing wage. So, the cost of the infrastructure is similar to any other infrastructure you would be constructing. However, in the states where we do have to pay prevailing wages, the cost of the infrastructure to be financed by the bonds will be higher.

Question 10: Who Manages the District?

That depends on what state we're in and what type of district we're looking at. In many instances, the district will be administered by the city. Alternatively, the districts are managed by third-party administrators, who are hired by the district, which typically happens in states where developers control the districts.

APPENDIX C

The Launch Sequence™

Carter Froelich

Phone: (855) 970-0003
Website: launch-dfa.com

THE LAUNCH SEQUENCE™

Launch Development Finance Advisors is a national transaction-based real estate consulting firm focusing on matters of public finance, solely on behalf of the private sector. We assist our clients finance infrastructure, reduce costs, and mitigate risks all with the goal of enhancing project profitability. Using The Launch Sequence™ we achieve these goals by breaking down each transaction into three distinct phases including Planning, Implementation and Management as illustrated below.

PLANNING

1. Conduct the D.O.S. Conversation®
2. Prepare The Eligible Cost and Fee Analysis™
3. Research Property Tax Rates of Competitive Development Projects
4. Prepare The Market Driven Bond Sizing™
5. Perform The RED Analysis™ (Reduce, Eliminate, Defer)
6. Prepare Development Impact Fee Credit Analysis
7. Generate Cash Flow and Proforma Analysis, Illustrating the Impact of District Financing
8. Prepare The Project Path & Plan™
9. Draft The Finance Plan™ for Presentation to the Jurisdiction

IMPLEMENTATION

1. Prepare and Utilize The Project Financing Checklist™
2. Add Favorable Financing Language to the Development Agreement
3. Prepare District Formation Application
4. Coordinate the District Formation Process
5. Assist with District Financing Agreements
6. Review Assessment Methodology (if applicable)
7. Review Appraisal and Market Study
8. Assist in District and Developer Sections of the Official Statement
9. Review Bond Documents for Clarity of Financial Matters

MANAGEMENT

1. Public Bidding Assistance
2. Monitor the Status of All Company Special District Activity through Launch Control System™
3. Track Reimbursable Costs through the Launch Reimbursement System™ (LRS)
4. Prepare and Process Reimbursement Binders using the LRS
5. Perform Developer Continuing Disclosure Obligation
6. Perform Lookback Diagnostic Reviews™ Related to Unreimbursed Construction Costs
7. As Appropriate, Manage District for Landowner/Developer (selected states only)

Arizona | California | Florida | Idaho | Nevada | New Mexico | North Carolina | Texas | Utah | Washington
Phone: (855) 970-0003 | Website: launch-dfa.com

TM and © 2022 LDFA, LLC. All rights reserved.

74

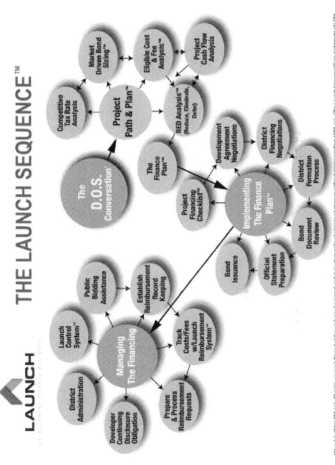

THE LAUNCH SEQUENCE™

LAUNCH

APPENDIX D

Special District Financing Advantages

The use of district financing creates a "win-win-win" scenario for the development community, the jurisdiction, and the homeowner as follows:

Private Sector Benefits

1. **Non-Recourse Financing**—In most cases, district financings are non-recourse borrowings to the developer, meaning that if the developer defaults on the bonds, the only recourse to the district is to foreclose on the property. The security for the bonds is either an assessment

lien on the individual lot or parcel, in the case of a special assessment or special tax levy bond; an increase in the *ad valorem* property taxes of the property contained with the special district, in the case of a general obligation bond; or the revenue stream created by an asset financed by the district, such as a water treatment facility or parking garage in the case of a revenue bond.

2. **Long-Term Financing**—Unlike traditional construction financing, which has a two- to three-year term, the typical term of district bonds ranges from twenty-five to thirty years.

3. **Reduces Equity/Third Party Borrowings**— The use of district financing to finance a portion of the project's public improvement costs reduces the amount of equity and/or traditional lending required.

4. **100% Debt Financing**—Conventional financing sources typically require equity contributions, whereas district financing is 100 percent debt financing. Additionally, no personal and/or corporate financial guarantees are required with district financing.

5. **Tax-Exempt Interest Rates**—District bonds are issued at tax-exempt interest rates and therefore are less expensive than the interest cost of borrowing from conventional sources (including potential lender participation).

6. **Interest Reserves**—Districts may borrow up to three years of capitalized interest to fund debt service requirements while the project is under construction. During the capitalized interest period, property owners within the district are not required to pay debt service on the bonds as this is funded by the district.

7. **No Acceleration Provisions**—Development loans typically have an acceleration provision in which the lender may foreclose on property for the entire loan amount, whereas with district financing, the district may only foreclose on the property for which the assessments and/or taxes are levied and unpaid.

8. **Accelerate Construction**—The use of district financing allows the developer to advance the construction of facilities, which may have had to wait until additional financing and/or project revenues were available with other financing approaches, such as impact fees.

9. **Additional Facilities**—The additional financing capacity provided by districts allows the developer to fund additional amenities or enhanced facilities, which otherwise may not have been possible, thereby potentially enhancing the marketability of the project to homebuyers.

10. **Impact Fee Credit**—To the extent that the developer is funding public improvements

through the district for which the jurisdiction is also collecting an impact fee, the jurisdiction must provide a credit against the impact fee to insure that new growth is not paying for the public improvement twice—once through the impact fee and a second time through the district.

Public Sector Benefits

1. **"Growth Pays for Growth"**—As districts typically only encompass a specific project boundary and not the entire jurisdictional boundary, special districts are well designed to ensure that growth is paying for itself without burdening the existing residents of the community.

2. **Preserves Debt Capacity of Jurisdiction**—The utilization of districts allows the jurisdiction to preserve its statutory bonding capacity for other public improvements.

3. **New Source of Capital Funding**—The use of district financings provides an additional capital funding source for the jurisdiction's financial toolbox.

4. **"Off Balance Sheet" Financing**—Typically, districts are separate and distinct from the jurisdiction in which they were established, and as such, the jurisdiction is not financially responsible for the debt obligations of the district.

5. **Competitive Advantage Among Public Entities**—The use of districts allows the jurisdiction that offers such financing to be more competitive than jurisdictions that do not.

6. **Fulfillment of Public Purpose Objectives**—The use of districts may assist the jurisdiction in accomplishing its public purpose objectives.

7. **Provision of Additional Amenities**—The use of districts may assist in the construction of public amenities which may otherwise have not been possible or may allow the developer to fund improvements to a higher quality standard.

8. **Faster than Impact Fees**—As districts may fund the construction of public improvements in advance of growth, they are much more efficient than impact fees, which arrive after growth has already occurred and can't be spent until they accumulate.

Homeowner Benefits

1. **Lower Home Prices**—As portions of the public improvement costs are financed through the district, it is not necessary to recover these costs through the home price, thereby allowing homes to be sold at a lower price point than that which otherwise would be possible.

2. **Additional Amenities**—Typically, projects that utilize districts have additional and/or enhanced public amenities (e.g., parks, trails, landscaping, open space) than non-district communities. These additional amenities create value not only for the jurisdiction and the master-planned community, but also for the homeowner's residence.

3. **Advanced Construction of Improvements**—The use of district financing allows the developer to install improvements in an accelerated manner that would not have been available otherwise.

4. **Reduce Operations and Maintenance Expenses**—Districts may fund operations and maintenance expenses of the project, thereby lowering HOA dues. As the operations and maintenance taxes are deductible for tax purposes and HOA dues are not, this provides an additional economic benefit to the homeowners.

Other Considerations

1. **Lender Consent May Be Required**—With the exception of revenue bonds, similar to regular property taxes, district special assessment/tax liens and *ad valorem* taxes have priority over any traditional lending. As such, it may be necessary to secure the consent of underlying lending

institutions to establish the special district. In our experience, obtaining lender consent has not been difficult, as most lenders understand that the establishment of the district will enhance the project's residual land value, and special district bonds will be issued over an extended period and often will be utilized to "take out" the lender's development loan.

2. **$5,000,000 Bond Issuance (District Sweet Spot)**—For an underwriter to garner the interest of institutional bond investors, a district bond issuance should be equal to or greater than $5 million. As institutional investors have hundreds of millions of dollars to invest, and the time it takes to place $1 million is the same as $100 million, they tend to look for larger transaction amounts, and $5 million is typically the lowest amount they will consider. It is preferred to sell district bonds to institutional investors as opposed to accredited investors, as it is easier to negotiate with three or five institutional investors as opposed to 300 accredited investors should bonds ever default and need to be restructured.

3. **Public Bidding/Prevailing Wage**—When considering the use of districts, one has to realize that using the district to construct or acquire public infrastructure may require the use of public bidding and the payment of prevailing wages. The requirements for public bidding

and prevailing wage vary from state to state and from district to district, so it is important to understand the specific requirements of your state and district.

While having to publicly bid the public improvements that will be financed by the district requires additional time and overhead, with the exception of the payment of prevailing wages in those states where this is required, public bidding should not result in a dramatic increase in costs. Generally, the contractor understands that the special district improvement work is a developer-driven project, and that if the contractor increases their pricing related to the district improvements, chances are the developer will not have them participate in the construction of other non-district improvements.

As it relates to those states that require the construction of public improvements through districts to adhere to the tenets of the Davis-Bacon Act, the cost of public improvements can increase between an estimated 10 to 30 percent.[2] If an infrastructure project has limited labor involvement, such as the paving of

---

[2] The Davis-Bacon Act of 1931 is a United States Federal law that establishes the requirement for paying the local prevailing wages on public works projects for laborers and mechanics. It applies to "contractors and subcontractors performing on federally funded

a roadway, the cost increase will generally be on the low end of the scale. On the other hand, an infrastructure project demanding a significant amount of manual labor to complete—such as the landscaping of a public park—could drive up the landscaping cost by as much as 30 percent. Accordingly, should your state require the payment of prevailing wage, you will want to fund non-labor-intensive public improvements through the special district as opposed to labor-intensive projects in order to minimize construction costs.

4. **Construction District vs. Acquisition District**—Districts can function as a construction district or an acquisition district. A construction district is when the district issues bonds to fund the construction of public improvements through the use of bond proceeds. In this instance, the construction contract is in the name of the district as opposed to the developer's construction entity. On a monthly basis, as construction takes place and draw requests are received, the district engineer will verify that the improvements that are the subject of the draw request have been constructed. Assuming there are no deficiencies in either the draw request or construction work, the district engineer will approve the draw for payment.

---

or assisted contracts in excess of $2,000 for the construction, alteration, or repair of public buildings or public works.

Once approved by the district engineer, the draw request is approved by the district board and the trustee is instructed to fund the draw request through funds held within the construction account.

In the case of an acquisition district, the developer's construction entity is often the contracting entity, and the developer funds the construction of the public improvements as they would normally do in the regular course of business. Once the improvement has been completed, the project will be inspected by the jurisdictional engineers and district engineer. Once the punch list items have been completed, the special district will issue bonds and "acquire" the completed improvement from the developer through the funds held within the acquisition fund.

Most districts are set up to do both construction districts and acquisition districts. However, given the constraints within the capital markets, more-and-more special districts are being established to issue bonds to fund the construction of public improvements through construction districts. The use of construction districts is also the most efficient and cost-effective method, as the developer is not having to incur financing costs twice—once through equity or a traditional construction loan and a second time through the special district.

5. **Operations and Maintenance Costs—** Districts can finance the construction or acquisition of the public infrastructure, but they may also levy *ad valorem* taxes or additional charges through assessment bonds to fund the ongoing operations and maintenance of public facilities within the boundaries of the district. While the rules related to the methods, timing, and amounts that can be funded vary from state to state, the ability to finance operating costs through a tax rate as opposed to an HOA fee can lower the HOA fee and allow the homeowner to deduct these tax payments from their income taxes. Such a tax deduction is not allowed for HOA fees.

Acknowledgments

My gratitude always goes first to my wife and lifetime partner, Bronwyn Froelich whose wisdom and counsel allow me to choose wisely.

Secondly, I would like to thank all our team members at Launch Development Finance Advisors and The Land Advisors Organization for their continued commitment to strive for professional excellence and to be a hero for the land investment, development, and home building industries.

Lastly, I would like to acknowledge and thank all our innovative, creative, and talented developer and home builder clients with whom we have been privileged to serve and collaborate with since 1986. I'm grateful for the opportunities and learning experiences that continue to grow and which always delight and surprise me.

About the Author

Carter is the Managing Principal of Launch Development Finance Advisors. Prior to the founding of Launch, Carter was the co-founder and Managing Principal of a national real estate consulting firm for 27 years. Preceding this, Carter was a manager in the real estate consulting department of the national accounting firm of Kenneth Leventhal & Company in both the Phoenix, Arizona, and Newport Beach, California offices. Carter is a Certified Public Accountant in Arizona, California, and Texas, as well as a former State Certified Real Estate Appraiser in Arizona. Carter holds a master's degree in Real

Estate Development from the University of Southern California and a bachelor's degree in Business Economics from the University of California, Santa Barbara.

Carter has over forty years of experience in the real estate consulting industry. Carter's area of specialty is in the formulation and implementation of land-secured financings for large-scale developments and the formulation of development strategies for large-scale master-planned communities.

Carter served as a City of Phoenix's Camelback Village Planning Committee member. Carter is a full member of the Urban Land Institute, Valley Partnership, and is a member of numerous Building Industry Associations in Arizona, California, Idaho, and Texas. Carter was the author of the 2008 and 2016 National Association of Home Builders' Impact Fee Handbook.

BLOCKCHAIN
VERIFIED IP™

Powered by Easy IP™

Your Next Steps with
Land to Lots™

ENJOY A COMPLIMENTARY 1-HOUR CONSULTING SESSION

MEET ONE ON ONE WITH CARTER FROELICH TO DISCUSS FINANCING OPPORTUNITIES RELATED TO YOUR DEVELOPMENT PROJECT.

SCHEDULE YOUR CONSULTATION TODAY AT:

ASKCARTER@LAUNCH-DFA.COM

Note: Projects should be 250 acres or more.

LAND TO LOTS™ PODCAST

LAND TO **LOTS**™
ACQUISITION, DEVELOPMENT & FINANCE

Carter Froelich hosts the Land to Lots™ podcast where he and his team help their clients finance infrastructure, reduce costs and mitigate risks all with the goal of enhancing project profitability.

LANDTOLOTS.COM